Phoebe Giannisi

CICADA

translated from the Greek
by Brian Sneeden

T0281879

A NEW DIRECTIONS PAPERBOOK

TRANSLATOR'S NOTE
Grateful acknowledgment is made to the venues in which some of these translations first appeared: *Parentheses*, the website of PEN America, *Two Lines*, and *World Literature Today*

Manufactured in the United States of America
First published as a New Directions Paperbook in 2022

Library of Congress Cataloging-in-Publication Data
Names: Giannisē, Phoivē, author. | Sneeden, Brian, translator.
Title: Cicada / Phoebe Giannisi ; translated from the modern Greek by Brian Sneeden.
Other titles: Rapsōdia. English.
Description: New York, NY : New Directions Publishing Corporation, 2022.
Identifiers: LCCN 2021043239 | ISBN 9780811230230 (paperback ; acid-free paper) | ISBN 9780811230247 (ebook)
Subjects: LCSH: Giannisē, Phoivē—Translations into English. | LCGFT: Poetry.
Classification: LCC PA5638.17.I1885 R3713 2022 | DDC 889.1/4—dc23
LC record available at https://lccn.loc.gov/2021043239

10 9 8 7 6 5 4 3 2 1

New Directions Books are published for James Laughlin
by New Directions Publishing Corporation
80 Eighth Avenue, New York 10011

Quickly the shedding progressed. Now, the head is free. The proboscis. Now the front legs gradually emerge from their casings. The body suspended in a horizontal position, legs upwards. Wings fledgling. Still creased, they look like the curved indentions of an arc. Ten minutes are sufficient for this first phase of transformation.
—Jean-Henri Fabre, *La Cigale: La Transformation*

SOCRATES: ... as we know, cicadas were human once, but after the Muses invented song some people were so entranced by the pleasure of singing that they didn't eat or drink, and before they knew it, died.
—Plato, *Phaedrus*

Stillness
the cicada's cry
drills into the rock
—Basho, tr. Robert Hass

Contents

Ecdysis

Leaves 3
Birthday 4
Weaving 6
Whirring Cicada 7
Cicadas 9
The Present Moment 12
Preparation 17
Poppy 19
Breath 20
Rites of Passage 23
Dream: Leda / Helen 25
Phaleron 27

Winged

You Me 31
The End 32
Rose Geranium 33
Touch 34
The Other 35
John and Yoko 36

Earth and Sky

Archilochus 39
High Road Low Road 45
Sublime Harmony 48
Depiction of an Original 50
Earth and Sky 51
Horse 54

Voicings

Fish 61

Word 62

Bed 63

Time 64

Places 65

Thought 66

Testimony

Eos and Tithonus 69

Tiresias 70

The Junk Dealer 73

The Car 74

Backyard 75

Homeless 76

Borrowed Brightness 77

Zeno's Paradox 78

Paros-Piraeus: Mini-History of the World 79

Via Egnatia 80

Platanidia 81

Stones 83

The Present Moment II 85

The Ferryman 86

Testimony 88

ECDYSIS

Leaves

Inside these articulations
the beginnings of language
outside of yes and no
inside only the I want
the soul with the body meeting
in all the openly
meteoric leaves
and now, see:
one of them falls slowly
to the earth

Birthday

Do the wings itch as they sprout?
When from the exit of the abdomen
you first raised your head
and pushing from the pain
sprang into the light
to cry out
were your eyes open?
Did you listen to their words
as they held, gently
your contorted body
gathered, legs tucked
and the day warm?
A woman giving birth
on the floor of her car—
is each growth
painful as the first?
Doesn't one grow
at the same pulse, imperceptibly?
Or is it after periods of stasis
when motion seizes you suddenly
and you grow and are unbearably changed?
Do you cast off the old
like the flower its petals
in the dew that you suck,
again and again?
Inhabited
by night's afflictions,
do you open your morning eyes

slantwise to survey the world?
You've gathered the stars, you hold them
in your hands, you scatter them
onto the earth and the sand
taller than ever,
you the tree
we fit inside your tiny shadow
lighter now, lighter

Weaving

The word by itself germinates
exists
beyond our decision for silence
every creature
on its path to the other
sings
but the threads of the planets
are distinct
no matter how closely they are woven
stutterings of half-raveled words
that though written
never mean what they say
or even what
you thought you meant to say

Whirring Cicada

I.

Only the voice desires
sweet voice thin as honey thick
dribbles and spills onto the earth below
Tithonus in his cage
whirring cicada
as the milk thistle flowers
as the burning state within a state
of summer detains each of us
the blaring cicada spills onto the ground
the voice
of the one who ceaselessly desires
and recites
from his own cadence relentlessly dizzying
like sirens drawing us imperceptibly to sleep

II.

Cosmic monotonous song of the cicada
each person according to their own mind
receives another melody and tone

Cicadas

I. Archilochus

Leaves of ivy play with the wind
apples redden on the branches
and then fall
the mouth fills with words
cicadas
blend with the noise of the cement mixer
and the ants
that walk along the wall
cutting a path entire armies
walking single file
to our dinner table
pears in the basket
you've spread out to ripen
you talk about partners
and the shield you tossed
into the game
say you were bravely defeated
through the ivy the sea
beckons you
distant bewildered turbulent

II. Winged words

for Mitsos

From drums in the viscera
a cicada screams
song of gathering
marked by weather fluctuations
and the dance of the other male
chant of premarital rituals
song of annoyances
croak of protest in captivity
when you catch its wing
seized a cicada by the wing
the summer my brother
ate a cicada
it fluttered
and screeched
alien voice from the fence
of the teeth
when the mouth opened
the cicada
took off flying

they call you cicada
you always face the sea

III.

The coming of age
we hope it will leave behind our voice
voice greater than life
because as Socrates says
cicadas
attendants to the muses
did nothing but sing
ceaselessly
to die in the end
fam-
ished
singing with the authority of an empty stomach

*in Aetolia today the children will tie the cicadas with a string and then
leave them on a branch to hear them sing*

(though in captivity
they die)

The Present Moment

I.

The wind carrying the voices
cools ruffles sleeves
travels to the edge of the dress
while over the asphalt
in front of the wheels
sparrow dances with the butterfly

II.

I open my mouth to speak
but my teeth clench
you a seashell
a hidden word
buried in the seabed
a mollusk
motionless in sand
with its antennae
twitching towards me

III.

Because the moment is inconceivable
not present at all
the "present"
"that which is here"
space in place of time
the tongue speaks in absence

IV.

Because meaning in language elides
my words
the baton
a pebble
borrowed
indefinitely they resemble another presence
before me
opening a path
and when the path is stepped on again
it is mine
and it is not
and when the path is stepped on again
it becomes a pit
to fall into

V.

For the hand that writes
the words
a voice speaks
shares assigns
bearing the thing that is most yours
even if it is borrowed
shares time
in fragments
shares prolongs
beyond all of us
stepping well and high
feet up in rhythm
music
towards the other
opening
towards the sun
pure longing
within absence
Apollonian dance

at the pier the moon
refuses its turn to come out

Preparation

Only then was I living
in the absolute present
while also preparing
the present
which belongs to preparation
I mean to the building of
each brick that is added
one by one
absolute now
before it stops
as
the sound of children's feet
racing
and the briskness of the doors'
opening and closing
the absolute present
for us
is the preparation
for them
of desire
and crickets have camped out
under the roof of the schoolhouse
perched in front of the microphone
to magnify their voices
and they serenade us
from their nook—
it's gone
it's gone

it's gone
what you were waiting for passed
without your noticing
it was already raining
raining
raining

Poppy

When from a distance and within
the body opens like the petals of a flower
as when the poppy bends
weightless head from the inexpressible
there are no rooms then
doors couldn't open
or even shut
see then
it whispers to itself
see the time Eros chose to take me
in the flowering sea
in the deep dark

Breath

I.

Breath of wind you blow and come
on the balconies at night as we sit outside
gazing at the sky
flowers trellising
a light whiff
as the butterfly flickers its wings
and standing on a flower
bees
suck juices make love
with their mouths and feet
sucking what's beneath
and the shifting weather
because who's to say
who can categorize elsewhere
in his collection
elsewhere the butterflies
the bees and plants
elsewhere the cats the goats
or the trees
elsewhere the mouth elsewhere the semen
elsewhere the stamen and vulvas
breath of wind
you who gently caress faces bodies
gradually naked
tossed into unshuttered night
with the sky's dome above the earth

wedged open
and in the joining we
slipped ourselves into their entwining
creatures of summer
sensually seeking a sweetness
and taking in
through the pores of our skin
open passages connecting outside and inside
pathways to the mind the heart
memory
all of us
tiny transmitters and receivers
in the great funnel
of the universe
spiraling endlessly
breath of wind breeze of the sea
voice whispering
I say take me
in your embrace
in your violence
and gently
let me go

II.

On summer afternoons
the soul's smoke
climbs and disperses into the previous
from other years
an accurate memory
waiting to be burned
inside the next
on this same day—August 20th
recalling
the heat the sweat
our cool respite in the water
in the now to be touched
in the eternal recurrence
of rebirth
plane trees lean down to the water
the crickets giant grasshoppers
organs of abundance
night
the stars
wading in the sky
each year
our vain return
to witness

Rites of Passage

I.

How do we go from one season—to another
one hour—to the next
slow and torturous and continuous
hence the rites of passage
all the ache
mixed with
all the fear
severing before from after

II.

You were crying—the clothes you wore
as a child
which constrained you
and which you'd been forced
to part with in order to
afterwards
in your new body
fall in love

Dream: Leda/Helen

I.

From a single egg
she waits
to be born
—she says—
without knowing what it means
because she was already born
because she had given birth also
first she would crack the shell
—she says—
into fragments
to break the membrane
and then you
o daughter would spring out
most beautiful of beauties
like every daughter
you'd emerge from the egg
to enjoy again the same pleasures
to make again the same mistakes

II.

You birthed the egg and you were the egg also
ripe flesh in spring
mumbling lullabies
for you and your daughter
how protracted and hard it is
to grow
to go from a child to a woman
to fly like a swan grieving
its former life

Phaleron

Afternoons my mother
would feed me
on the sands of Neo Phaleron
next to us the trawlers were leaving to fish
—what's a trawler really?
is it a boat that fishes with a net?
all that we can name by knowing
and all we name without knowing
language
blind
it catches them with its net on the seafloor
brings to light
fish mollusks oysters seaweed junk
with no name
within the person who grows up watching
the sea before them vanish
and the pile of debris that hides
the horizon
and the island across the way

WINGED

You Me

You giving me without asking giving me because you want to give without even knowing you give giving me effortlessly when I never expect it but also perhaps when I do and when I expect without knowing it or your giving this knowing before I do in my place wanting what I want before I realize I want it or wanting what I want because you are more me than I am wanting together the same thing or wanting what the other will give us when they give it giving together before we can think of it or want it and for it to be a shared desire or to be ready to receive it to have desire in place of the other when you tell me we're going to do this I know you'll like it and we do it and I like it more than I thought I would maybe I like it more because you thought of it and not me but you thought of it on my behalf before I could you were me before I was myself because the two together are something else that goes further than our separate I's a double me a double you

The End

I wonder what'll become of us in the end the end for both of us what we are now what can words say about it I don't know the words I don't know what words say words that we say aren't ours the words for us don't belong to us the words spoken are always foreign often I think the end has come though you're close to me your body feels foreign no I mean your body isn't foreign but your soul is different somehow not mine I know how it feels when it's mine when I recall it I think perhaps the god has loosened the knot and tears begin to seep down to the eyes I stop them when they touch the brim I stop them because you're here even though I want you to know I'm crying for the end because I hope the end isn't real but an idea a moment of unfaithfulness between one and two between myself and you still I want you to prove it to me and since nothing has been spoken I return everything to its place again I begin to wonder again I recall again how it was I found again how things might be I remember that paradise existed in the infinite of the sea under the vastness of the sky one facing the other and one's eyes in the other's eyes one's body in the other's body the other's soul in their body and in their soul though everyone knows how first creations end

Rose Geranium

A plant in a pot a pot beside a table a table with chairs with people a plant in a pot in front of a road followed by sand a beach then sea the plant is green intense green I don't know the names of the green when you cut it and rub it between your fingers the plant has a smell its smell is intense I can't describe it smells and colors are never described except in metaphors the plant is used in sweets for its aromatic properties down the street people walking the sounds of forks and knives laughter conversations the sea crashing on the beach spraying the plant in the earth beside the steps beside another aromatic plant named *verveine* we call it *louiza* in Greek the French also drink it in a tea like chamomile a sedative at night I drank it also before sleeping when I decided I'd be tranquil always but then chose the agitation the ecstasy in life the ego that ricochets within the body the body within the world naked filled with emotions mutable yet always the tranquility returns it returns so we can live we die continuously until at last we become eternally tranquil

Touch

Where's the cell phone did we bring it you asked and began to look through the bag the bag that was always filled with stuff filled with everything in disarray tangled up with one thing inside another with your arm deep inside the hole you rummaged the dark sanctorium I think it's in here you said though I'm not sure because I just barely touched it if it was really what I was looking for and so we continued on our way why should what you touched not be what you're searching for I said what you touched and didn't see is always what you search for you have to trust your touch as much as your vision I said maybe even more I thought touch and smell are closer to memory closer to truth because they're nearer to the body than vision to smell to touch I have to be in close contact one on top of the other only one on top of the other the truth

The Other

I looked at the photograph many times I look at it often and also the other photographs from back then your face our faces back then the faces of other owners the faces of other people is it because it was a different time I asked it's because it's the past you said it's because then was then I said then with someone else you weren't the you I know you said I look again at the photograph the gaze is different the laughter more open the gaze more tender I say to myself the world for you was lighter then and the eyes you were looking into weren't mine I said you're kneeling the angle is from above you're smiling calmly with joy with the sea behind us you used to belong somewhere else I belong somewhere else I'm unrecognizable a stranger you said men don't enjoy looking at old photographs women like it I said they're always looking to find what will hurt they're always looking to find what will hurt not only in what will happen but also what happened what happened is far away from us now you said and yet it's not it's always near I said what happened is gone but may return the stranger may come back again inside the one you love the hidden stranger a ghost waiting to rise to the surface to take on another gaze another laughter turning to face someone else and you become him and I'm not her

John and Yoko

Lying face up in bed with that photo of John Lennon and Yoko Ono the one taken from above do you remember ten years ago in that other house that other time it was still the same position the ceiling looking down at us what does one ceiling see that the other doesn't if only for a moment we could be each one from its particular point of view different from the outside from the inside two identical snapshots ten years apart two snapshots with two different pairs one of John alone looking at Yoko from above and the other of Yoko with the same John ageless immortal dead and she alive mortal older looking into the mirror of a photograph over millions of years couples intertwined lying face up couples facing the ceiling the sky and lying there

EARTH AND SKY

Archilochus

In one of his books, Athenaeus preserves
a verse by Archilochus that goes like this:

"As for the figs of Paros—famously
called *aimonia* by the locals—Archilochus
commemorates them with this line:
ἔα Πάρον καὶ σῦκα κεῖνα καὶ θαλάσσιον βίον."

ea Paron kai sika keina kai thalassion bion

In English: *goodbye to Paros and those figs and life on the sea*
Eight salvaged words, preserved by choice:
Someone (Athenaeus) wanted to commemorate someone else
    (Archilochus)
who in turn commemorates something (the figs).
The objective of this preservation is memory, the opposite of
        forgetting.
Through writing, what one knows and retains
is preserved.
And so this verse passes to our hands.
Eight words of alliterating *k*'s and *a*'s.

The first word: *ea*
In English:
goodbye
And now back to Greek
say goodbye to it—to Paros
calling to mind of course the last line of Cavafy's poem

"The God Abandons Antony":
and say farewell to it, the Alexandria slipping away from you.

And though the first word in the verse that sets the tone—*ea*, an
      imperative—
was translated *goodbye* in English
really it's more like
"I leave I abdicate I omit I defy I relinquish I
abandon I ignore I neglect." *Leave it*—then—*Paros
and those figs and life on the sea*
or even
abandon it, Paros.

The same word, *ea*,
is said by Odysseus to Achilles
ἀλλ' ἔτι καὶ νῦν παύε', ἔα δὲ χόλον θυμαλγέα
i.e.
"stop now and abandon
this rage which injures your heart."

ea, the second person imperative of *eao*
brings us directly to the question:
who is speaking, and who are they speaking to?
Someone (we guess the poet) addresses
in the second person imperative
someone else who is leaving Paros
or must leave it
and telling them to say goodbye to it, to leave it, to abandon it.
And the other could also be the poet
(a monologue then: "abandon it" to oneself)
or even the reader, I mean, us.
And maybe the imperative can be taken to mean the inversion

of a particular situation:
"leave it (the place where you now live)"
and maybe it also conveys
acceptance,
acceptance of finality,
acceptance of the inevitable to come.

ea: the first word, which sets the fragment's tone
abandon it, it doesn't fit you
or on the contrary
say goodbye to it even though you don't want to
say goodbye to it because you must.

Second word: *Paron*
That which must be abandoned is the island, Paros.

Third word, also the sixth: *kai*
A connective conjunction. It joins with Paros,
with those figs, and with the life on the sea.
Used twice it also means: not only, but.

ea Paron kai sika

Fourth word: *sika*
Fig: fruit of the fig tree
but also, fig: female genitalia, according to my dictionary,
or as Aristophanes put it:
his fig thick and stout
where hers is sweet

ea Paron kai sika keina

Fifth word: *keina*
keinos: poetic Ionian version of the demonstrative pronoun
ekeinos
Demonstrative pronoun demonstrating a person or thing
far away in place or time
yet already mentioned.
Not just: the figs
but those figs *there*, not here.

From far away the speaker
POINTS AT THEM WITH HIS MIND,
like Vamvakaris when he sings
"of the Creator, there"
and points at god
far away and not here.
Those figs, with emphasis on *those*, those far away,
aren't here anymore
those you can gaze upon from far away,
those you remember, nostalgic already,
or those that have passed, or the reverse:
those you didn't want, which afflicted you,
those goddamn figs over there.
Together with the first word, *ea*,
the fifth word *keina*
restores emphatically the tone and tinge
through its *e* and *a*.

ea Paron kai sika keina kai thalassion

Seventh word: *thalassion*
thalassios: adjective, meaning "of the sea."

ea Paron kai sika keina kai thalassion bion

Eighth word: *bion*
bios: life, the way of a life.

Bios thalassios is the life of the sea,
the life next to or in or along the sea,
the life bearing characteristics of the sea,
the way in which one lives in the sea,
or the manner in which it provides food.

The fragment's diverging interpretations
arise from the rich tone and tinge,
whether the figs are vaginas—an erotic life corresponding
to life on the sea, gladness—or suffering or exhaustion,
or the figs are being eaten,
and the edible fruit of late summer is associated
with life on the sea as
food, seafood, and fish.

We are free
to choose our own interpretation every moment,
for this verse that causes us
to go away and leave
because the second person imperative can always
mean us
—in the open fields of Paros,
sea and land,
paradise or affliction, in August.

ea Paron kai sika keina kai thalassion bion

Always an admission, a salutation, of *those*.
Say goodbye to it, to Paros, not only to its figs but to life on the sea.
Abandon it, Paros, and those figs and life on the sea.
Abandon it, Paros, with its figs and life on the sea.
Abandon it, Paros, with its loves and its life along the sea.
Abandon it, Paros, figs, and sea.
Leave it, Paros, and those vaginas, and the afflictions of the sea.
And say goodbye to it, Paros, and those figs and life on the sea.

Or, better yet:

ἔα Πάρον καὶ σῦκα κεῖνα καὶ θαλάσσιον βίον.

High Road Low Road

I.

For partnership between equals
pairings of opposing powers
male female
sky earth
north south
cold warm
up down
light dark
right left
Heraclitus answered:
high roads and low roads are the same

High roads and low roads are the same
not in the sense
as I once thought
that the exhaustion of going uphill and downhill are the same
but rather
that uphill and downhill are accorded the same value
ascent and descent
good and evil
if made into an equation
$+(\alpha) = -(\alpha)$
male equals the opposite of female
with equal absolute value
add them together and you get 0
or even

from that same unit
two split fragments
one's curve matching the other's
so that when joined
we'd have a perfect sphere—with the crack
Aristophanes mentioned
of the two severed from the beginning
and through Eros
perfectly fitted again

here is the sphere
made from two halves
if you consider it in terms of composition
the sign of the Tao is completed
two joined without division
and should it appear like antithesis
we have Strife
semiosis difference limitation
war
the strong onto the weak

II.

Instead of making opposites be equal Empedocles
preferred to complicate the union
and perfect assembly
of two parts
and the intertwined
members roots plants animals
and from their union to originate
a plethora of composite disparate data
deviant blends of cyborg creatures
Empedocles's addition doesn't end in subtraction
no invisible glue
from each joint something Other
goes missing
something entirely different
a surplus of subplots and array

Sublime Harmony

"And the white bones exquisitely dovetailed
by the glue of Harmony"
naturally Empedocles
with a name like *everlasting glory*
the glory
rubbed off on the ground
where we stand
and so on
speaking for the white bones
which somewhere along the way Harmony "dovetailed exquisitely"
he must have come across
the white skeleton
of a perfect Being still in its joints
Exposed and Polished by the elements
a Being Older and Stranger
or some Being he knew well
in both its living form
and the one it retained
after death cleaned it to completion

(he was crazy about free will
Empedocles
with his feet rooted in "glory"
meanwhile of course
Heraclitus
was bored to tears
because while the other
labored tirelessly

to set up his construct of variations
painstakingly he
Hera's glory
in a single sentence delivered
each time
his erudition
condensed
contentious
ironic
dark
the Dark Truth requires a Clenched Ass)

Depiction of an Original

One
simple
to be described
yet distinct
and were you to add
one to one
once more an original one will come out
1+1=1
each time another child
distinct
the same complexity
simple
to be described
words say something less
and something more
hair blond brunet curly eyes blue brown
strong knees spread arms

Earth and Sky

I.

Clouds have enveloped the mountain
losing its peak in the sky
which like an embroidered dress
covers everything
encircling with its body
the body of the earth
humming ceaselessly
and us mortals below
with friendship joy
joining limbs
like our works when we look upon them
and when they are complete

Strife stands apart
parting one into many

II.

Sky dark
sea gray blue
trees acquiescing to gusts of wind
everything obeys the sky
bowing, rooted to the earth
only a ship in motion
has volition to resist
a machine's volition
invisible to us
propels it onward
life is that which leaves
motion volition
forward
what parts the volition of others
from the sky?
what parts it
from its roots in the earth?

III.

Is the departure
the journey
just a working
of sky?

if fate is the sky
one which
comes from somewhere overhead
one which
like war or earthquakes
finds you.
The name of the unknown was always Sky.

Horse

Starts to prepare to begin to uproot
the invisible rungs of the ladder
spiraling into the sky
they close their eyes for a moment
breaths drawing in the double dance

are they singing now?
or perhaps dancing?
traveling
galloping in emptiness
in the desert's vast
empty spinning infinite?
on what road?
galloping over what?
is one the other's horse?
or rather
is one the top and the other the bottom
as they ride mounted
on the same horse-
body
to carry them at this speed?
only seemingly governed by its rider
when it's they who belong to it
it steps on the ground and runs
while the deluded
with their digits dangling

in the air
forgo spurs or saddles

thought action shifting from here
to there to here following
limbs perceiving motion
fingers edges openings mouths
surfaces
signs
whatever it seeks it finds through touch
the mind's focus leaps frenzied
from one here to the other
joining here there here there there there

open
to what touches
closed eyes
open to see
then closed open closed
when they open perhaps they encounter
the face
when they open they encounter
another's eyes, yours
perhaps they peer into their depths
gaze piercing the soul
to the bottom to find only emptiness?
on their road
do double gazes
meet?
or is it that they encounter
the other's contact
with the infinite far away?

now a pause
the gathering of powers the onset
of a wind damp but not chill
the air of winter caressing
the sky weighted with clouds
from the quiet gray sea
swollen
the soft earth anticipating
it rests
the sound of the roll of the waves
the sound of the beyond
the beyond over there
touches the flesh the skin
in the kitchen a pot is boiling

II.

In stillness Hannah says only in stillness
can a human think
only in stillness can he accept the world.
I think back: I invert revert return
going over it again I reiterate
I invert the earth with the plow I plow
I revolve in spirit I meditate consider:
when the soul in itself reminisces
when the soul reminisces itself inside itself
this I do in stillness
as our steadfast horse
reminisces about the tender grass tufted from earth
and with the plow of my mind I dig and dig
the soil
I dig to recover some old roof tile some old song
that grew before my stepping here before me
I kept it in a drawer
when they tried to take it from me I hid it deeper
when the soul inverts the soil of itself
inside itself
when the soul inverts
the soil inside it
rare double root
you inhaled
air and light

VOICINGS

Fish

Wherever I stand I see the sea the sea through the window the sea through the mirror through the window the sea in the clouds in the sky the same as the sky in the sea a bird a seagull flies and leaves the sea through the window of the mountain the mountain through the sea in the sea beneath the sea in the surface of the sea behind the sea beyond the sea the earth's sweat the sky's teardrop inside the boat beneath the boat and along the horizon's curve the sea the horizon inside the fish I eat but the fish never noticed doesn't know the sea doesn't know the horizon always present inside the sea the fish doesn't have a balcony

Word

From my house I look out at the sea existence is a thing of places places in the world physical and otherwise places with and without the intangible places otherwise transitory places in this world are stable they have a given width and height they have geography when I cease to exist I don't have a place anymore they say the words *I* and *here* come from the same root yet the place of memory persists even Achilles best of the Achaeans dies and is left to remain without his death his place only temporary yet with his death it perpetuates it becomes permanent our place only lasts in the memory that exists after us but how can memory exist without the knowledge of the one I met that one is able to remember me remember my body my voice more mine than how I appear and afterwards when the one who knew me is lost in turn I'll be lost too everyone is lost after death with the death of friends only a sort of biological continuation persists through time a nameless immortality

Bed

How do we give a funeral for this animal how do we bury it after having lost it never to be found again we loved it it was there next to us in the house sometimes it sighed sometimes it farted it was an animal cinnamon-colored with brown eyes it looked at us sad its tail wagged sometimes the animal wanted to go for a walk it looked to the fireplace it laid its braided head on its front paws the animal was female in its psyche there was a butterfly with heavy wings and in its psyche it read our own reddish animal cinnamon-colored it took part in battles it took part in sorrows in took part in joys meals dinner conversations always together as we grew up so much that we forgot it so much that we grew even older so much and before that we also shook the petals and before that we died it was a dog her name was Daphne

Time

Our connection to others is the time we give them said the man
in the movie when he was about to die or maybe he said the time
we give is all we've got I don't recall exactly maybe he could've also
said that time is the only thing that exists nothing but time said the
dying man and then you start realizing how little time you gave here
or there and maybe when you were or weren't giving that time you
realized the same thing differently I mean the meaning of presence
and the meaning of absence we always say it's distance that matters
and not closeness distance that creates desire whereas closeness
erases your desire and my desire this is one way yet one could argue
another way if the intensity of my presence and your presence can
be equalized if time is not just a quantity but an intensity though
time is defined by quantity what is a mortal's time but the quantity
of their existence this countable time of a mortal's lifespan is mor-
tality this lifetime of closeness and distance time apart and time
together is all that's given to us spending our procession through the
world is only this wasting of time time which without knowing its
final quota arriving from elsewhere is given to be mindlessly spent

Places

—Yet there are things we do not decide said the man who was about to die meaning of course his own death—but you can't die said the woman who loved him there must be something we can do let's go to America she said—there's nothing to be done he told her and with this knowledge the knowledge of his death which is equal to the knowledge of our nonexistence our nonexistence between the constant existences of others and automatically equal to being forgotten and automatically equal to our own replacement by other persons other persons everywhere and in every possible place persons replace without actually replacing because each person is singular this being the definition of person yet even still the replacement exists maybe it's the replacement of the role I mean the replacement of the place that is mine yet someone else's yet still my person no one else's and with that knowledge the protagonist selects in the arrogance of despair his own replacement his replacement in all the places that he once occupied and who he believes won't be able to replace him in the end because he still believes he's superior we always believe we're better than our replacements

Thought

Death doesn't exist says Epicurus because while we live we're alive and don't know what death is and later when we die we don't exist anymore so death doesn't exist for us he said this because he knew that we know we are going to die and this makes us different from other animals his words and thought are valid because of course if animals possessed thought they'd be in our position too because they'd have knowledge of the future thought means projection projection means changing one's place in time or in space according to Nietzsche the joy of animals is tied to lack of memory and so the present is only the present meanwhile a human sees the present through the past alone yet also sees the past through the future I wonder can a human see the present through the present what does it mean for a human this moment where she lives this hour where she lives after it's already been forgotten this moment this now was only ever from the outset irrevocably dead

TESTIMONY

Eos and Tithonus

It was Eos who prayed
for Tithonus—a mortal—not to die
begging that his days become
numerous
as the grains of sand emptying from her hand
and the Sibyl asked the same
to Apollo, yet—
now they seek their own ghosts
in the pauses
between grains of sand
in the bodies they embrace
eyes closed
seeking in vain
a single drop
—Nightingale and Cicada

Tiresias

I.

Lying in the sand
a snake
licks my face
behind so many eyelids
eyelids of silence
I glide from creation's
slightest crackle
the cloud's chasing
the tree's shedding
the thought's shimmering
the wave's scintillation

II.

Oars:
boat's wings

III.

Rose with the thousand eyelids
pomegranate
with the thousand seeds

IV.

Cicada eaten by ants

V.

Houses by the sea
light air of September
distant noise of the saw
garden shadows
a woman in black sweeping the road
pomegranates, plane tree, cypress
angelica
a man with a dog
underneath the olive trees
sofas cast-iron chairs
from the '60s and '70s
backyards of vacation houses
wealth within so little
gravel, flatbread, and pines
nostalgia with black wings
crosses from beyond the sea

The Junk Dealer

"Kitchens washing machines old fridges
old storage units I'll empty"
the junk dealer who buys words I wonder
will he buy the light?
(the words are coins
he scrubs them in water
to polish them
so they'll shine as they fall)
yes, he bought the light
a dime
and goes about singing
proclaiming the same and the same
binding past with future
brimming with longing
and they clang
inside the old jalopy
the pieces of scrap the old lamp's skeleton
the spring

The Car

We got rid of the old car
that for so long had born us in its viscera
like an animal
a sagacious donkey
it accepted us it ferried us unharmed
observing our squabbles our kisses
our children growing up
now when they unload scrap
at the ports
from the old cars made in china
our mouths clogged
we inhale the motes
of our own rust

Backyard

From the backyard facing the mountain
pra-pra pra-pra pra-pra
the engine of a boat
conveys the sea into the room
like warmth into the bedsheets
a body
missing a while now

Homeless

In the morning in the room
we found a bird fluttering
confined
with the window open
it kept speeding up to fly
and hitting the ceiling

nests
the homeless homes of birds
each with its own sky
each with its own freedom

Borrowed Brightness

"Lit with a borrowed brightness, wandering the earth"
—Parmenides

I can't see her
she's hidden herself
light suffuses the sky
like night's zipper left open
filtered blue over the mountain
a man hears
but doesn't listen
even to his own voice
touching the edge of the universe
shoulders broad
eyes full
of glaucous deep blue gray light you
sky
you rinse us
not knowing our fleetingness
whatever you let drop appears new
inside the radiant ancientness
the man hears
the woman opens her palm with its blueprints
far from thought
wind caresses the houses
filtered blue brightens the expanse
eternal moment of gaze
without purpose

Zeno's Paradox

Night
where blue horses of the moon
graze
where the roaring
of the vast flower of the sea
opens one by one its thousand petals
where in stillness the distant
murmur of the mechanical crane
echoes unloading from ships
containers of sand for making cement
you wait
you bite your lips curl your tongue
you have no voice
you wait to come again to find yourself
and go back to the beginning
mortals
so that you may leave
up on the highest branch of the tree
your apple
there where nobody
neither your hands
nor the insatiable mouth of time
can ever reach

Paros-Piraeus: Mini-History of the World

On reliefs inside the large graves
you can observe in fine detail
how they caught ducks with huge nets on the Nile
how they drove water to the fields with sluices
how they swam in the water by kicking their feet
how they ate onion bread at the table with their hands
how the cook would cut
vegetables into slices with his knife
and fry the onions in a pan
how the mothers would call out at dusk
to draw their children home
how giant magnolia flowers would fall suddenly
slowly white on the dirt
how the cicadas stubbornly kept singing
even after sunset
how the sea was calm at morning and restless by noon
his fingers struck the keys so violently
the crickets reminded us
of this late summer
that soon ends

Via Egnatia

—What did you see and what brought you sudden pain?
which was the stabbing knife?
—the glued-together heads of the lovers
drinking the other's mouth
with no quenching
a bridge
suspended over the valley
Arachthos
far from the wheels
water leaks from everywhere
the sky
the roof of our bus
licks, wets the mountains
each bend a new rivulet of mud
and another tunnel
beyond the curb
alone
traveling
the pain in freedom—the unknown destination
over an abyss—the foreign teenager
clinging to the back of the seat
outside, two houses gently touch
shoulder to spine, pressing
like sheep
trees signal
the presence of the ravine

Platanidia

Were you to pass fallen leaves
on the road you'd see
waves licking
women in pairs on the benches
from the courtyard where a table overlooks the sea
you'll see men lined up to fish
tearing off on old mopeds *pra-pra*
fathoming the sea with rods
(though she gives them little)
leisurely the men
only pretend to work
waiting like the rest of us
for the unexpected to appear
a red fishing boat
coloring the wave
I walk along the shore
among the scent
of bitter mud
mud of the field mud of the seabed
scent of evening primrose
soaked yard
yelping dog
a waiter with a tray
crosses the street
a solitary woman
a cricket
I have no secrets from you

which is why I'll invent
a stone filled with feeling
a sea still as a lake
a sky

Stones

I.

I wanted to be able
to become a stone
a mute stone deprived of language
and each night
bereft clear-voiced bereaving
for years each night singing
until all feeling drained out
and exhausted I burrowed
into the dreams
of the youth who grieve for the future

II.

Our dream gathered
and spit us out polished
in the night
without tears
without the depth of touch
the morning couldn't find space
to bring its light
across to the other side
on the riverbank stones
one by one
open their eyes

The Present Moment II

And sudden
as the eye catches
a bird in flight
flitting darting
something alights

suddenly and discovers you
the absolute present
that which finds you
without your asking
the unexpected

and shortly afterwards or perhaps
simultaneously the desire
to shake off to step out
into the future
to seek something undiscovered

to repeat the unrepeatable
nostalgia
the first sensation that immerses
each creature
after it leaves to be born

The Ferryman

I.

You saw the ferryman
alone
slicing silently
the sea
leaving behind as he slices
that which always remains open
what does he see as he calmly progresses
towards the outside
he hears
the sky
shimmering
in the inexpressible light of water
what does he see
the mortal
he rehearses at death
wind
the absolute horizon
only the leaves of the olive tree know
what lies inside him
—a rehearsal in light

II.

Rehearse in light
person human mortal
within what floats
cast out for your shadow in the faraway mountains
so small or so large
as you progress unmoving
you imagine you've abolished it
while on solid ground
from where you can be seen
the sound of wheels
relentlessly treading
the stones even as they roll
lightly on the soil
deeply rooted in absolute dark
ferryman sealed inside a shell
we're yours
"better to be eaten by fish than by worms"

Testimony

You, cicada
you don't exist anymore
I'm coming to find you
I'm combing the tamarisks
the sea exhales
from wind
a plastic bag hanging
from the branches
you, cicada
you don't exist anymore
the black eyes of summer
are closing their eyelids

CICADA

ALSO BY PHOEBE GIANNISI

Homerica